THE P...
ABUNDANCE

Praying the Prayer Of Jabez
By Dr. MORRIS CERULLO

Foreward

I never cease to be amazed with the way God hides golden nuggets of truth in His Word for His servants to find.

The story of Jabez is more than a nugget; it's a gold mine of wealth.

My prayer is that your faith will be strengthened as you read these pages. Please be sure you read the final chapter because it contains one of the most significant truths of the whole story.

Dedication

I dedicate this book to my darling Theresa,
my partner in life for more than fifty
wonderful years.

To our Partners throughout the world

I challenge you to pray this prayer every day as Theresa and I do. It will open the door to manifold blessings in your life. Learn the words and pray them from the depths of your heart.

THE PATHWAY TO ABUNDANCE

Praying the Prayer Of Jabez

Table of Contents

Chapter One 1
"Oh that thou wouldest bless me indeed"

Chapter Two 11
"And enlarge my coast"

Chapter Three 21
"And that thine hand might be with me"

Chapter Four 35
*"And that thou wouldest keep me from evil,
that it might not grieve me"*

Chapter Five 49
"And God granted him that which he requested"

Chapter One

"...Oh that thou wouldest bless me indeed,"

Neatly and discreetly tucked away in the midst of an almost endless list of names are two of the most profound and provocative verses in the Old Testament.

Profound in that they reveal a simple approach to the Father; yet provocative because they cut a swath across traditional religiosity.

Religionists dissect this prayer as selfish and carnal since the prayer is without due regard for others. After all, haven't we been taught that we must always consider others before ourselves if we hope to receive an answer from God?

Herein lies the simplicity and the beauty of the man Jabez and the prayer he prayed.

"And Jabez was more honourable than his brethren: and his mother called his name Jabez, saying, because I bare him with sorrow. And Jabez called on the God of Israel, saying, Oh that thou wouldest bless me indeed, and enlarge my coast, and that thine hand might be with me, and that thou wouldest keep me from evil, that it might not grieve me!" 1 Chronicles 4:9-10

The Hebrew word "honourable" has both a positive and negative meaning in the positive sense, it means rich, abounding, noble etc.

The negative means; more grievously afflicted, sore, dim.

So I had to ask myself this question, "Which meaning fits the man, Jabez?"

In all honesty, given his name and the kind of prayer he prayed, I am convinced the negative meaning of the Hebrew word "honourable" is the one that most adequately describes Jabez.

At birth he was given a name which interpreted means; "Sorrow, Distress, Grieve, Pain." Now you need to remember, in Bible days, names meant something, so from the day he was born he was known as Sorrowful or Painful or the Grievous one.

He grew up with a name that marked him for the worst things that could possibly happen to a person.

If you ever saw a man who went about with a cloud raining on his parade, it was Jabez.

The name alone was enough to give him an inferiority complex.

He was no doubt the last one to be chosen for childhood games, after all, who would want "Sorrowful" as a teammate?

If there ever was a born loser it was the man by the name of Jabez...but he prayed.

His prayer was divided into four sections.

First he prayed: ***"Oh that thou wouldest bless me indeed."***

Let your mind grasp this picture. Here is a man who has all his life lived on the down side. Sorrowful, lonely, heartsick, shunned by others, poor, in need, perhaps he was even dim witted, but one day he called on the God of Israel for a blessing.

Mark it down; when anyone calls on God, in faith, something good is going to happen.

Forget about where you came from, forget about your mental capacity, forget about what others say because none of those things move God.

Our Heavenly Father is not looking for the bright, beautiful, popular, rich, and glamorous of this world, He is looking for men and women, boys and girls who pray.

He is looking for those who pray with purpose, design, plan and objectivity. He is looking for modern-day "Jabezs" who will defy the odds, discard what others say and think and reach into the realm of divine possibilities. This is not a lesson on possibility thinking; it's a lesson on believing for that which is impossible, moving the immovable, reaching the unreachable.

Jabez could have settled for a life of sorrow and pain. That was his name and he could have lived up to it fully. He could have taken up residence in Sad City, on Self pity Lane, but he didn't. He prayed.

His prayer was not filled with the usual fluff, froth, flowery words and repetitious phrases we've become accustomed to hearing people pray. Rather, it was simple, straightforward and to the point.

"O that You would bless me indeed!"

I am not intimating or suggesting that we should not be concerned with the needs of others or that we should only pray for ourselves because the heart of a true

Christian is always concerned for others. What I am saying is, that it is easier to be a blessing when you are blessed than when your own needs are weighing you down.

We wage war from the vantage point of our strength not our weakness. Tennis champions don't challenge world heavy weight boxers to bouts in the ring. Perlman the great concert violinist does not suit up on Sunday to play football; he knows where his strengths lie. The same is true for you. Your strength is not in poverty or want, sickness or distress; you are in the best possible position to bless others when you are blessed, prospered, healthy and happy.

Sorrowful, sad and dejected Jabez realized he needed to change more than his address. He needed to change his destiny.

Change Begins With An Attitude Adjustment

Let me stress the importance of a "right" attitude. Men and women caught in the quagmire of negative thinking must make a mental and spiritual adjustment.

But how does an individual make that all-important adjustment?

Through faith!

The author of the book of Hebrews said it most succinctly in his dissertation on faith:

"But without faith it is impossible to please and be satisfactory to Him. For whoever would come near to God must (necessarily)believe that God exists and that He is the rewarder of those who earnestly and diligently seek Him (out)."
Hebrews 11:6 AMP

Jabez didn't just pray to any god; he called on the God of Israel. He was not concerned with being politically correct or he would have prayed an amalgamated prayer that went something like this:

7

"Oh thou mighty force, who is known by many names, Baal, Molech, Pharoah, (today it would be Allah, Buddha, Shinto), we are unworthy of asking for anything from you blah, blah, blah."

Thank God Jabez was not concerned with being politically or "religiously" correct! He called on the God of Israel, the true and living God and he asked specifically to be blessed.

Never underestimate the power of specificity! When you speak to God, know what you want and why you want it. If you need healing, He is the Great Physician.

If you or someone you love needs salvation, Jesus Christ is the Savior of the world. His blood can make the vilest sinner clean. And...there is no limit to His loving forgiveness. He wants every man woman and child of every race, creed and color to be saved.

Do you want financial blessings? Then:
*"Always remember that it is the Lord your
God who gives you power to become rich..."*
Deuteronomy 8:18 TLB

And...please keep in mind that you are not
limited to salvation, healing or finances.
God's blessings are as limitless as your
imagination. If I may borrow a line from a
world famous book: "If your mind can
conceive it and your heart can believe
it...you can receive it!"

I believe the glorious God of Heaven is
searching the earth today for men and
women upon whom He can pour out His
bountiful blessings. Men and women who
will dare to pray in simplicity and in faith.
Men and women who will not be afraid to
say with Jabez of Old Testament fame:

"O that You would bless me indeed!

Make this positive statement of faith with me!

I confess Jesus Christ is the Ruler of Heaven and Earth. Because He is, I have every right to claim the full benefits His death on Calvary provided for me. God the Father raised Him from the dead and I am a joint heir with Him.

Just as the Father has bestowed life upon Him, He bestows life upon me so that I may boldly say; I am a child of the King!

Chapter Two

"And enlarge my coast"

As noted in the previous chapter, Jabez did not lisp a feeble petition to whatever god happened to be on duty that particular day. No…no…no, he boldly called on the God of Israel and made his needs and desires known.

First he said:

"Oh that thou wouldest bless me indeed"

Then he became very explicit with his request! "And enlarge my coast." This phrase is most interesting because of its fantastic implications in the language it was written in. The two Hebrew words I want you to see "ENLARGE" and "COAST" unlock the secret to this portion of his prayer.

The Hebrew word for "enlarge" is "rabah" which has several descriptive words. Let me share a few of them with you: increase, abundance, be in authority, excel, exceedingly, be full, great, gather, take in, multiply, nourish, have plenty and tucked in the midst of all these wonderful descriptions is the word "give".

I'll come back to that in a moment, but first, let's talk about the various words that fit together like beautifully colored threads in a priceless tapestry, the whole of which make up the word, "enlarge".

The first time I read the meanings of the Hebrew word "rabah," my heart began to sing a new song. I saw the bigness, the greatness, just how unfathomable Jabez's faith was. That man was not day dreaming while looking at a Sears & Roebuck catalog. He was taking a calculated risk. He was daring to become what no one in his family had ever been. He was breaking the mold, shattering the bonds, destroying the yoke, cutting the cords and stepping out on a new uncharted path.

Jabez was in effect changing his name from Sorrowful to Delight, from Pain to Comfort, from Dejected to Courageous.

His prayer was not to increase his sorrow, suffering and pain, which has been the common teaching of some churches in this day and time.

I hate to think of the many Christians who have been taught to thank God for sickness, sorrow and defeat because sufferings draw them closer to the Lord.

The Word teaches us…"in" all things, not "for" all things, to give thanks! In the midst of our deepest trials we are to continually praise God. That's because praise gives strength to the inner man; but we certainly do not give praise for sickness, disease, heartache, poverty, want, lack or distress. We don't give thanks to God for any of those maladies, because none of them come from God.

The Word boldly declares:

> *"Every good gift and every perfect gift is from above, and comes down from the Father of lights, with whom there is no variation or shadow of turning."*
> *James 1:17 NKJ*

And the Word also proclaims:

> *"...His divine power has given to us all things that pertain to life and godliness, through the knowledge of Him who called us by glory and virtue."* *2 Peter 1:3 NKJ*

Jabez was well acquainted with sorrow and pain from infancy, he had grown up with that moniker hanging about his neck. He had been the butt of cruel jokes by virtue of the name he was given.

His prayer was not, "give me strength to endure one more day," but "turn my darkness into light." When praying, "enlarge my coast," he was not saying multiply what I already have... but change

me from the loser I am to the champion
Your divine purpose designed me to be.

Earlier, I told you that I would come back
to the word that to some, could seem out of
place in the description of "rabah" the
Hebrew word for enlarge. It isn't however,
an accident that "GIVE" is included in the
fabric that makes up the total picture of
"enlarge." It is one of the most vital
aspects of enlargement.

The secret of true success is bound up in
this one fantastic word, which expresses the
very nature of the Father, Son and Holy
Spirit, the triune being of God.

Look again at the most beloved of all New
Testament verses:

> *"For God so loved the world that He
> gave His only begotten Son..."*
> *John 3:16 NKJ*

Jesus Christ gave His life and He is the
Giver of life! John 10:10

The Holy Spirit, also known as the Comforter, gives power–glorious, supernatural power to the Believer! Acts 1:8

God was, is, and will always be, a Giver. Giving is as much a part of His nature as love! God loved…so He gave! To bring it closer to home we can truthfully say God loves…so He gives!

Every man, woman, boy and girl who wants to grow, enlarge, and succeed in life must of necessity take on the nature of God. Taking on His nature means adopting "giving" as an integral part of life.

The second word in this portion of Jabez's prayer that I want you to see in the Hebrew is "ghebool." Eight different words are used to fully describe this word…territory, boundary, landmark, border, coast, limit, quarter and space. Let me see if I can paint a word picture for you.

Jabez was saying to God, "I want You to extend my territory; take off the limits.

The space where I am living is too small;
my quarters are too cramped. Enlarge the
borders of my thinking, my faith, my
living, and my giving!" "I don't want to
be bound by the landmarks of smallness
any longer. Enlarge my coastline to
include the region of prosperity, the land of
plenty, the mountains of abundance and the
grounds of greatness."

"I want to sow precious seed in the soil of
rich return, eat at a table overflowing with
succulent morsels of a bountiful harvest,
and drink the sweet waters of success."

Jabez was weary of being "Sorrowful," and
tired of being "Painful!" He knew that in
God there was more to life than barely
getting along on barely having enough.

He could have wasted his life struggling
with the stigma of who he was and where
he came from. He could have bathed in the
tub of self-pity and fed his soul with sour
swill in the "No-Hope Café." He could

have given in to being one more statistic in
the loser's almanac…yes…he could
have…but he prayed,

"And enlarge my coast!"
With that one simple phrase he raised his
eyes from where he was, who he was, and
where he came from, and caught a glimpse
of the greatness of his God.

Jehovah, the God of Israel was not mired in
the muddy ruts of nothingness; He was not
bound with chains of desolation, nor
clothed with destitution. His God was high
and lifted up; He was clothed in majesty
and honor, and compared to His brightness,
the sun was pale.

The gates of hell must have trembled as a
simple man of sorrowful beginnings shook
off the bands that bound him; put on a
garment of righteousness, and took on the
image of his Heavenly Father.

Jabez the "Painful" was given a new song.

Gone was the woeful tune of tears and sorrow,

Gone was the fear and dread of tomorrow,

Golden shafts of light filled his heart,

The God of Israel gave him a new start!

Take me O Lord, from where I am with my handicaps, my troubles and pain to the place of Your blessing. Strip from me the rags of failure, free me from my miserable past. I desire to abide close to You, because, in You there is life Abundant!

"And enlarge my coast!"

Make this confession of faith with me!

God is bigger than any sin, sickness, disease, heartache, or sorrow that I may have. So I will not be afraid of anything the enemy brings my way. I believe the Lord is enlarging my coast, my territory. Because of Christ living in me I am more than a conqueror!

Chapter Three

"And that thine hand might be with me!"

Stop! Look at the bigness of Jabez's faith as he utters these words, "that Thine hand might be with me!" This statement is especially meaningful when you realize that through the teaching of the rabbis, he was aware that it took only the finger of God to write the Ten Commandments in the tables of lapis lazuli stone.

This can be an exhilarating truth for your soul from the Holy Spirit. Jabez asked the God of Israel, the Creator of the Heavens and the Earth to become more than an abstract, unapproachable, out-of-touch God to him. He was asking for a close, one-on-one relationship akin to that which the patriarchs Abraham, Isaac and Jacob had with God.

The words, "that Thine hand might be with me" are tied directly to the impartation of blessings from the fathers to the sons.

Let me give you some examples!

While the Bible does not speak specifically of Abraham laying his hand on Isaac to impart the inheritance. It does show however, that he took Isaac to Mount Moriah, bound him and placed him on the altar. According to the Law, the hand of the priest was upon the head of the sacrifice when the animal's throat was slit; so when Abraham stretched forth his hand to take the knife, his other hand was upon Isaac's head. At that moment he could have imparted the full inheritance to Isaac.

The Word is much clearer in its account of Isaac imparting God's eternal blessings on Jacob. Likewise Jacob when laying his hands on the sons of Joseph, purposely crossed his hands to favor the younger son above his older brother, who according to birth should have received the greater blessing.

Never underestimate the power or the potential blessings that can be bestowed on an individual through the laying on of hands.

But it doesn't stop there! There are other vital aspects of this portion of the prayer that we need to explore. For example, protection! Jabez no doubt saw the hand of God as a shield from the attacks of the enemy; as the Psalmist said:

> *"Show the wonder of Your great love, You who save by Your right hand those who take refuge in You from their foes."*
> *Psalms 17:7 NIV*

> *"You give me Your shield of victory, and Your right hand sustains me; you stoop down to make me great."*
> *Psalms 18:35 NIV*

Jabez saw the hand of God as a mighty weapon and a conquering force:

"We have heard with our ears, O God, our fathers have told us, what work thou didst in their days, in the times of old. How thou didst drive out the heathen with thy hand, and plantedst them; how thou didst afflict the people, and cast them out. For they got not the land in possession by their own sword, neither did their own arm save them: but thy right hand, and thine arm, and the light of thy countenance, because thou hadst a favour unto them."

Psalms 44:1-3

He saw it as protection in times of trouble:

"Though I am surrounded by troubles, you will bring me safely through them. You will clench your fist against my angry enemies! Your power will save me."

Psalms 138:7 TLB

Jabez saw God's hand as the Source of Deliverance:

"But for those who fear you, you have raised a banner to be unfurled against the bow. Selah. Save us and help us with your

right hand, that those you love may be delivered."　　　*Psalms 60:4-5 NIV*

He trusted the hand of the Lord to satisfy:

"You open your hand and satisfy the desires of every living thing."
　　　　　　　Psalms 145:16 NIV

And the strength of His hand to withstand any enemy:

"Thou hast a mighty arm: strong is thy hand, and high is thy right hand."
　　　　　　　Psalms 89:13

When I repeat this prayer; which I do daily, this portion: "and that Thine hand might be with me" reminds me of a powerful statement Jesus made when He was accused of casting out devils through Beelzebub the chief of devils. Christ said to His accusers:

"But if I cast out demons with the finger of God, surely the kingdom of God has come upon you."　*Luke 11:20 NKJ*

You and I can rely on the immutable words of Christ when we pray this portion of the prayer. Jesus said:

"My sheep hear My voice, and I know them, and they follow Me. And I give them eternal life, and they shall never perish; neither shall anyone snatch them out of My hand. My Father, who has given them to Me, is greater than all; and no one is able to snatch them out of My Father's hand."
John 10:27-29 NKJ

When we pray, "And that Thine hand might be with me," a sense of security should fill our heart because we are safely planted in the hand of the Father. Nothing, nothing, nothing…neither men or angels or demons from hell can snatch us from that place of safety.

With His hand about us we are preserved and protected, sheltered and shielded from the onslaughts of the enemy; His hand makes us impregnable!

What an incredible blessing it is for His children to know that we have His hedge of protection, His strength, His unconquerable power keeping us, around the clock, every day of our life.

This portion of the prayer, "…that Thine hand might be with me," echoes so graphically the masterfully penned words of the Psalmist David:

"Shall I look to the mountain gods for help? No! My help is from Jehovah who made the mountains! And the heavens too! He will never let me stumble, slip, or fall. For he is always watching, never sleeping. Jehovah himself is caring for you! He is your defender. He protects you day and night. He keeps you from all evil and preserves your life. He keeps his eye upon you as you come and go and always guards you." Psalms 121:1-8 TLB

When I speak the words, "…that Thine hand might be with me," in my spirit I see two visions: In the first vision I see the mighty, the majestic, the all powerful, the warring, the conquering hand of God that is always surrounding and protecting me.

The second vision, is that of a loving Father tenderly caressing His child. I see Him touching and healing, comforting and guiding, blessing and restoring. How many times have you seen a child holding tightly to a father's finger as they walked together? It gives a child a great sense of security when they feel the power and strength of a father's hand. And, so it is with you and me when we walk in the blessed assurance that the hand of God is with us.

When Jabez prayed his wonderful prayer he didn't have the decided advantage that you and I have of reading the dozens of places that refer to the hand of God and the manifold blessings His hand provides for His children.

A very interesting truth to take note of is: the same hand, which overflows with blessings, also metes out judgement to the ungodly.

The book of Daniel gives us a great example of this truth. King Nebuchadnezzar had taken the children of Israel captive.

When his army subdued Judah, they ransacked the city and carried the gold and silver vessels of worship from the temple to Babylon and put them in the king's treasury where they were kept.

After Nebuchadnezzar's death, Belshazzar his son inherited the throne. He was an impulsive man who had no regard for the God of Israel or for the vessels that were dedicated to Him. In a show of pompous pride and self-glory Belshazzar made a great feast for a thousand of his lords.

When you read the story it appears that it was nothing but a drunken bash. Amid their revelry the king made a fatal decision. He called for the gold and silver vessels from the house of God that he and his lords, his wives and his concubines might drink wine from them and praise the gods of gold, silver, brass, iron, wood and stone.

He took those vessels which were dedicated and consecrated to the living God of Heaven and desecrated them by praising false gods.

"Suddenly, as they were drinking from these cups, they saw the fingers of a man's hand writing on the plaster of the wall opposite the lampstand. The king himself saw the fingers as they wrote. His face blanched with fear, and such terror gripped him that his knees knocked together and his legs gave way beneath him."

Daniel 5:5-6 TLB

Frightened by what he had seen the king called for the wise men to come in and read the writing on the wall, but it was to no avail. No one could read the words. God had written in the language of the Holy Spirit so the interpretation would have to come from a man acquainted with Him.

At the suggestion of the queen mother, Daniel was summoned to the banquet hall and asked if he could read the writing and make the interpretation known to the king.

When Daniel saw the writing, God immediately gave him the meaning of the words but before he explained them to the king he revealed one of the great truths of all time. King Belshazzar, he said, *"...the God who holds your breath in His hand and owns all your ways, you have not glorified."* Daniel 5:23 NKJ

The words that spelled the ultimate destruction of the wicked king should bring great peace to every child of God. It is comforting to know that He holds our very breath in His hand.

As you repeat the words of Jabez, *"and that thine hand might be with me,"* you are surrounding yourself with the strength, the power, the might, the protection, the security and the glory of Almighty God. His hand holds the very breath of life.

But there is more!

God is not an amputee!

Be assured in your heart that when you repeat the words, "and that Thine hand might be with me," you are going to get more than a detached hand. Because God is not an amputee! You are going to get all that God is! His hand with you means you have Him in all His glory, His entire splendor and all His majestic being. Whisper the words in the ears of your children and grandchildren, speak them when you rise up in the morning and let them be on your lips throughout the day.

Let it be your prayer when you give the day back to God in the evening, "and that Thine hand might be with me," Say it with all your heart and mean it with all your soul…

"And that thine hand might be with me!"

Make this bold confession of faith with me!

I am strong because the hand of my God is with me. I will not walk in fear of man or things, for You are beside me giving me strength for my journey today.
No weapon that is formed against me can prosper for the hand of my God is a shield about me and I am safe in Him!

Chapter Four

"And that thou wouldest keep me from evil, that it might not grieve me!"
There are four distinct areas we need to implore God's mercy and ask Him to keep us from evil.

First is our spirit!

Every Christian must recognize that the greatest battles we fight are in the spirit. Your spirit man is in a constant battle against evil forces and must be reinforced daily by the Holy Spirit in order to maintain your position of faith and strength.

Paul wrote: *"For we wrestle not against flesh and blood, but against principalities, against powers, against the rulers of the darkness of this world, against spiritual wickedness in high places." Ephesians 6:12*

In another place he wrote: *"...the weapons of our warfare are not carnal, but mighty through God to the pulling down of strong holds" II Corinthians 10:4.*

Since we do not wrestle against flesh and blood, and the weapons of our warfare are not carnal, then the first thing on our agenda is to be covered by the blood of Jesus Christ and be built up in the spirit.

Mark this truth and store it in your best place of remembrance: your flesh is incidental to the devil. He is after your spirit! The greatest battles you will ever fight are to keep your spirit in harmony with the Lord. When your spirit is attuned to the Holy Spirit you are a dangerous enemy to the rulers of darkness. It is then and only then that you are a force to be reckoned with.

To say the devil doesn't attack physical bodies would be ludicrous because he does! But that is not his primary goal; he attacks the body as a secondary target with the hope that a weakened body will lower the resistance in the spirit.

When we say, *"that thou wouldest keep me from evil, that it might not grieve me!"* we are talking first about our spirit man which must be renewed day-by-day, (II Corinthians 4:16). We are saying keep me clean: keep me pure, keep me holy that evil might not grieve me.

The second major area of concern is the mind!

Several years ago I wrote a best seller on the battle for your mind.

Let me explain!

The devil works tremendous deception on the mind trying to confuse men and women regarding the will of God. If he can convince you that God is so busy running the universe that He can't be bothered with your individual needs, then God is no longer the personal Savior you placed your confidence in and therefore cannot be trusted to uphold any of His divine promises.

You and I must guard our minds! We do this by guarding what our eyes see, our ears hear and the words that come out of our mouth.

Can a person watch pornography and not be affected mentally? And not just pornography! The daily soap operas and countless other television shows are filthy and are designed to pollute the human mind.

David said:

"I will set nothing wicked before my eyes..."
Psalms 101:3 NKJ

Why was the Psalmist so adamant about what he saw? He knew that the eye is a gateway to the soul.

What about your ears, how edifying can it be to listen to the vulgar lyrics of some of today's music, that not only blasphemes the name of the Lord but incites hatred toward the police, drives barriers between races and degrades women?

I'm not saying that you should never listen to anything that's not Christian music, but be careful about what you put into your ears lest it get into your spirit. The Bible teaches us to guard what we hear because faith comes by hearing the Word of God.

We need two spiritual sentries on duty at all times to protect our minds from being assaulted through our eyes and ears.

The third area for the prayer, *"that thou wouldest keep me from evil, that it might not grieve me!"* is the words we speak. Notice what Jesus said: *"For by your words you will be justified, and by your words you will be condemned." Matthew 12:37 NKJ*

Your words are powerful for both good and evil, that's why it is so important that you learn to confess and speak only that which blesses and edifies the hearer, including yourself because you, more than anyone else, hear the things you say.

Your words carry the seeds of eternity in them. Your words can build up and strengthen or they can tear down and destroy. So speak positively, speak constructively, speak graciously always remembering that your words have creative ability living in them.

Am I espousing some mindless mantra that teaches mind over matter? No! What I am saying is that your mind is fertile soil that must be properly cultivated and sown with good seeds or the evil one will come and plant seeds of unbelief.

What you see, hear, and speak will have a lasting affect on you and those around you so pray earnestly, *"that thou wouldest keep me from evil, that it might not grieve me!"*

The fourth area of vital importance to this prayer is finances!

That's right...finances!

Every child of God must guard their finances with prayer and vigilance lest they violate the principles set forth in both the Old and New Testaments. God's command to us is, *"Always remember that it is the Lord your God who gives you power to become rich, and he does it to fulfill his promise to your ancestors."*

Deuteronomy 8:18 TLB

God entrusts riches into the hands of His children that we might enjoy life but it is important to remember that everything belongs to Him. We are the caretakers of His blessings.

Jesus gave us a powerful illustration of this great truth when He told the story of a very prosperous farmer and the false illusion that his farm and the bumper crop in the fields were the result of his ability alone and that he had control of the wealth that had been entrusted to him. Here is the story as told by Christ:

*"...The land of a rich man brought forth
plentifully; and he thought to himself,
'What shall I do, for I have nowhere to
store my crops?' And he said, 'I will do
this: I will pull down my barns, and build
larger ones; and there I will store all my
grain and my goods. And I will say to my
soul, Soul, you have ample goods laid up
for many years; take your ease, eat, drink,
be merry.' But God said to him, 'Fool! This
night your soul is required of you; and the
things you have prepared, whose will they
be?' So is he who lays up treasure for
himself, and is not rich toward God."*

Luke 12:16-21 RSV

When I read this story I am reminded of a
wealthy farmer in the Midwest. The man
was a Christian who loved the Lord deeply
but he had missed one important truth; he
thought that his diligence and long hours of
sweat and toil were the reason for his
success.

It was with a great sense of accomplishment he showed his farm to a visiting minister. As they looked out across the lush fields, the fat cattle, his beautiful barns and magnificent home, the minister exclaimed, "Oh, how good the Lord is to give you such a bumper crop and this incredible herd of cattle; God is so good!"

Annoyed by the profuseness of the preacher's praise to God for what he considered the result of his hard work the farmer said, "Before you get carried away I want you to know it was me, not God, on the tractor every morning before daybreak plowing the fields and planting the seed that produced these crops."

Realizing he had touched a nerve with the farmer, the minister apologized. "I meant no offense to you, it's obvious that you've done an extraordinary job and you are to be commended for all your labor."

"But... please tell me one thing, what did you do to make the sun rise each morning, and how did you control the wind and rain because it's evident that these crops received rain at just the right time and how did you manage to be with each cow when it was time to calve?"

Tears ran down the farmer's cheeks as he suddenly realized that the Old Testament promise was being fulfilled in his life for it was God who had given him the power to get wealth. And quite unlike the New Testament "fool" he began to give God praise for his success and larger portions of the bountiful harvests.

There is no question as to Who owns this world for the Word boldly proclaims: *"The earth is the Lord's, and the fulness thereof; the world, and they that dwell therein."* Psalms 24:1; I Corinthians 10:26-28, the title deed to this earth is still in His name. God is the rightful owner of everything and He has made us caretakers of His divine bounty.

When you pray, *"that thou wouldest keep me from evil, that it might not grieve me!"* it is for these four distinct areas: spirit, mind, words and finances. Keep in mind that you can walk in victory in each of them.

"That it might not grieve me!" is the last portion of this wonderful prayer. Jabez had a keen spiritual insight of what evil does to an individual. The pain, grief and suffering it inflicts on an individual is beyond comprehension. Since evil comes from the evil one it bears his resemblance, carries his mark of destruction and will eventually share his penalty.

In summation to the final part of the prayer, *"that it might not grieve me!"* may I quote a phrase from the beautiful hymn of the church, "What a Friend we have in Jesus, all our sins and griefs to bear." Jesus Christ bore our sins and carried our griefs to Calvary. It is through His sacrifice, His atoning grace that we are shielded protected and kept from the evil one.

To Him alone be glory in the Church now and for all ages to come.

"And that thou wouldest keep me from evil, that it might not grieve me!"

Join me in this proclamation of faith!

O Lord Jesus, it is through You alone that I stand in victory over the forces of evil. It is Your power that keeps me safe and gives me the wisdom to make the right decisions.

I will not walk in fear or trepidation for You are constantly beside me guiding and directing my life for success and total fulfillment.

Chapter Five

***"And God granted him that which
he requested."***

By now you have no doubt noticed that I
enlarged the first word of the chapter name
on chapters two, three, four and five. I did
it to emphasize the importance of the little
conjunction, "**And**."
When you read Deuteronomy 28 you get
the impression that Jabez used the first
thirteen verses as the basis for his prayer.

Let me take you there, it's like taking a
journey to the "Land of **And**."

*"**And** it shall come to pass, if thou shalt
hearken diligently unto the voice of the
Lord thy God, to observe and to do all his
commandments which I command thee this
day, that the Lord thy God will set thee on
high above all nations of the earth: **And**
all these blessings shall come on thee, **and**
overtake thee, if thou shalt hearken unto the
voice of the Lord thy God. Blessed shalt*

*thou be in the city, **and** blessed shalt thou be in the field. Blessed shall be the fruit of thy body, **and** the fruit of thy ground, **and** the fruit of thy cattle, the increase of thy kine, **and** the flocks of thy sheep. Blessed shall be thy basket **and** thy store. Blessed shalt thou be when thou comest in, **and** blessed shalt thou be when thou goest out. The Lord shall cause thine enemies that rise up against thee to be smitten before thy face: they shall come out against thee one way, **and** flee before thee seven ways. The Lord shall command the blessing upon thee in thy storehouses, **and** in all that thou settest thine hand unto; **and** he shall bless thee in the land which the Lord thy God giveth thee. The Lord shall establish thee an holy people unto himself, as he hath sworn unto thee, if thou shalt keep the commandments of the Lord thy God, **and** walk in his ways. **And** all people of the earth shall see that thou art called by the name of the Lord; **and** they shall be afraid of thee. **And** the Lord shall make thee plenteous in goods, in the fruit of thy body,* *and in the fruit of thy cattle, and in the fruit of thy ground, in the land which the Lord sware unto thy fathers to give thee. The Lord shall open unto thee his good treasure, the heaven to give the rain unto thy land in his season, and to bless all the work of thine hand: and thou shalt lend unto many nations, and thou shalt not borrow. And the Lord shall make thee the head, and not the tail; and thou shalt be above only, and thou shalt not be beneath; if that thou hearken unto the commandments of the Lord thy God, which I command thee this day, to observe and to do them:"* Deuteronomy 28:1-13

I made the word "and" bold each time it was used in those thirteen verses to help you grasp the significance and the power of this simple little conjunction.

At no time did God use the word "or" if He had, you would need to make a choice as to which blessing you want. Reading His promises as He enumerated them opens the door for you and me to receive not one, not two or three, but every blessing He promised.

Notice, God said: *"Blessed shalt thou be in the city, and blessed shalt thou be in the field."* That tells me that it's okay with God for His children to have more than one home. One in the city and another in the country.

He said: *"Blessed shall be the fruit of thy body."* Women all over the world who were barren have claimed these words and received the miracle of conception.

But God wasn't finished yet! He said: *"**and** the fruit of thy ground, **and** the fruit of thy cattle, the increase of thy kine, **and** the flocks of thy sheep."*

The Lord tied all the wonderful promises of those thirteen verses together with the little conjunction "and" to make His blessings

full and abundant to His children. Make a
mental note of this dynamic truth: the
blessings God has promised are not
reserved for heaven. I assure you that
heaven is going to be far superior to
anything we have on earth but that doesn't
mean we are simply marking time until we
enter that fair city in the sky. God has
provided everything we need to live a
happy prosperous life here on earth. He did
not intend for His children to be homeless,
broke, penniless paupers.

One of the great promises of the Old
Testaments is, *"But the meek shall possess
the land, and delight themselves in
abundant prosperity." Psalms 37:11 RSV*

In the Sermon on the Mount Jesus said it
this way, *"Blessed are the meek: for they
shall inherit the earth." Matthew 5:5*

Many people have been misdirected into
thinking that Christ was speaking only
about Heaven when He delivered that
wonderful message about the beatitudes.

My question is: why would the meek inherit the earth after they have gone to Heaven? The time for the meek to inherit the earth is now!

Let me make this point clear, I believe in Heaven. I believe there are streets of gold and walls of jasper just like the Bible describes and I know that Heaven is my final home. But I'm not there yet and until the day that God calls me home, I plan to live life to its fullest. God's Word does not teach me that I am to go about in threadbare clothes with holes in the soles of my shoes. I am a blood-bought child of God.

My point is, if ten theologians were asked to analyze the prayer of Jabez without knowing its source, nine of them would declare it to be a selfish, self centered prayer that God would not listen to and certainly not answer because the man prayed only for himself.

God however, saw the desire of a man's heart and responded to him in the grandest fashion. The Word says,

"And God granted him that which he requested."

I encourage you to find a place in your daily devotions to repeat this wonderful prayer. Let the words find lodging in your spirit; let them flow from your heart as you seek the face of God in your times of intercession. If you will, I believe the God who answered the cry of Jabez will also answer you.

God is a God of great abundance and He has offered to share it all with you and me because we are His children. As you lift your voice to Him in earnest prayer you will find Him very near. He is your God and He delights in answering the cry of your heart. Remember, it is His good pleasure to give you the Kingdom.

Learn this marvelous prayer and say it from your heart!

"Oh that thou wouldest bless me indeed, and enlarge my coast, and that thine hand might be with me, and that thou wouldest keep me from evil, that it may not grieve me!"

Don't forget to include the final line!

"And God granted him that which he requested." **(I Chronicles 4:10)**

Join me in making this bold confession of faith!

As God's child I lay claim to the promises set forth in the Word. I will not accept second best in my spirit, mind, body or finances. It is my Father's good pleasure to give me the kingdom and I will accept nothing less.

Sin has no place in me because of the blood of Christ!

Sickness has no place in me because He bought my healing!

Fear has no place in me because He said: "Fear not!"

Poverty and want have no place in me because I am a joint heir with Jesus Christ!

MORRIS CERULLO WORLD EVANGELISM
San Diego: P.O. Box 85277 • San Diego, CA 92186
(858) 277-2200
E-mail: morriscerullo@mcwe.com
Website: www.mcwe.com

MORRIS CERULLO WORLD EVANGELISM of CANADA
Canada: P.O. Box 3600 • Concord, Ontario L4K 1B6
(905) 669-1788

MORRIS CERULLO WORLD EVANGELISM of GREAT BRITAIN
U.K.: P.O. Box 277 • Hemel Hempstead, Herts HP2 7DH
44 (0) 1 442 232432

For prayer, call: 1-858-HELPLINE
HELPLINE FAX: 1-858-427-0555
HELPLINE E-MAIL: helpline@mcwe.com

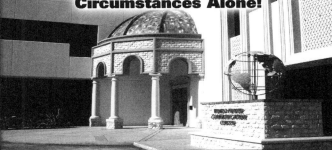

ABOUT THE MINISTRY OF MORRIS CERULLO

Dr. Morris Cerullo, President
Morris Cerullo World Evangelism

Morris Cerullo's accreditation for ministry is in itself quite formidable: a divine, supernatural call from God to preach and evangelize when he was only fifteen years old, and over half a century of experience as a pastor, teacher, author of more than 200 books, and worldwide evangelist.

Many honors have been bestowed on Morris Cerullo, including honorary doctorates of Divinity and Humanities, both by academic and spiritual leaders and heads of state around the world in recognition of his achievements and contributions to global evangelization.

Dr. Cerullo is respected and revered by millions around the world including over one and a half million Nationals trained through Morris Cerullo's Schools of Ministry. His ministry outreaches include:

- **The Morris Cerullo Helpline Program** – a major television cable and satellite weekly hour long, prime time broadcast reaching out to hurting people in virtually every nation on earth.

- **Schools of Ministry** – training national pastors, ministers and laypeople to reach their nations for Christ through mass evangelistic crusades.

- **Mission To All The World** – reaching the entire world, region by region, with Schools of Ministry, crusades, television prime time specials local Schools of Ministry designed to cover every village, city and town in every region in the world.

Dr. Cerullo has made a tremendous impact on the destiny of the nations of the world. He has sacrificially dedicated his life to helping hurting people and to train others who will take the saving message of God to their own nations.

We Care

Morris,

I am sending you my most urgent prayer requests. Please pray for my needs:

_____
_____
_____
_____
_____
_____
_____
_____
_____
_____

❑ Enclosed is my love gift of $/£ _____ to help hurting people through the ministry of Helpline.

❑ Please tell me how I can become a Helpline Circle of Hope member to help keep Helpline on the air as I make a monthly financial commitment.

❑ Please send more information including the benefits and resources I'll receive as a Circle of Hope member.

Name _____
Address _____
City _____
State or Province _____
Postal Code _____Country _____
Telephone (_____) _____
E-mail _____

Mail today to:
MORRIS CERULLO HELPLINE
U.S.: P.O. Box 85220 • San Diego, CA 92186
Canada: P.O. Box 3600 • Concord, Ontario L4K 1B6
Europe: P.O. Box 277 • Hemel Hempstead, Herts HP2 7DH

✂ (Tear off and mail this today!) ✂